ONE STEP to FREEDOM

Leaving the Habit/Mindset You Hate
to Live the Life You Love

WORD & SPIRIT
PUBLISHING

Copyright 2023 by Mark Delaney
Website: markdelaney.com
Email: mark@markdelaney.me

ISBN: 9781685730239

Credit for the artwork: Paul Joy
Email: handdrawntoday@gmail.com

Published by Word and Spirit Publishing
P.O. Box 701403
Tulsa, Oklahoma 74170
wordandspiritpublishing.com

Dedication

I want to dedicate this book to my wife, Adena.
I love words. I love finding words to describe
complex things. But as I sit to write this page,
I do not have the words. My wife, Adena, has
been right beside me throughout my entire adult
journey. I do not have the words to articulate who
she has been to me. What we have experienced
together is indescribable. Her impact on me
cannot be measured. If it were not for her grace
and love for me, this book would not have been
written. It may be my hands on the keyboard,
but it is her hand on my shoulder that has
emboldened me to write these words.

I also dedicate this book to my three kids.
Matthew, Kelsie, and Andrew have each been a
gift to my life. To be called their dad is an honor.
Matthew, Kelsie, and Andrew: Thank you for
believing in me and loving me. Your lives inspire
me. Each of you has made an impact on my life
more than you can know. I am proud of each of
you. You never have anything to prove to me.

I also dedicate this book to my grandchildren. As
I write this, Ruby and Jace are about nine months
old. I am watching you learn to crawl right now. I
pray this book will someday help you to run free.

Acknowledgments

There is a simple thought that moves me daily, and I believe it with all my heart: When common people take uncommon steps with other common people, miracles become common. I feel that is the story of my life. So many common, yet extraordinary people have played a role in my common life—and miracles have happened! I wonder if I should even include this page because I will certainly leave people out—especially because there are many people who have impacted my life without me even knowing it. But I cannot publish this book without speaking of these people who have been a gift in my life.

MOM AND DAD: your faithfulness paved the way for fruitfulness in my life. You both are what is right about life.

MY SIBLINGS—Erich, Kara, Sharon, David, Tim, and Ryan—how can we know the ways in which we impacted each other? I could speak about each of you. But I want to declare how proud I am to be your brother, and I further declare that our best days are yet to come!

DIANA PELHAM: your life served our lives. The greatest form of love is to serve others. Thanks for the love.

RANDY PELHAM: I showed up at your house for Christmas to meet you, and I told you I was marrying your daughter. You supported us and believed in us all the way through.

MY EXTENDED FAMILY: your names are many. I'm humbled by your presence in my life. I am sobered as I wonder if I have been all that I could have been to you.

Early Childhood

MR. PITTENGER: You made school interesting. I'll never forget the spelling test in the dark or the time you paddled me for throwing snowballs.

MR. RILEY: You allowed students to dream and invent in the classroom. You were the only basketball coach I ever had. I still remember the game in sixth grade when I made two shots. I couldn't wait to see you at school the next day to see if you would say something about it. You did! And it made my day. Those were the only baskets I ever made while playing on a basketball team.

TINY ADAMS: You coached me in baseball. With my level of athleticism, it was not easy. I recall you driving the team around in your van. You once had to miss a game because you were a fireman. I pitched that game and did great. I couldn't wait to see you after the assistant coach told you how I did. You were excited about it—and that was the only time I ever pitched well playing on a baseball team.

RICHARD HARDESTY: When I was a teenager, you took an interest in me. I didn't think I mattered much, but you made me feel like somebody.

High School Years

MRS. PATTERSON AND MRS. RANKIN: You are the only teachers in high school I can even recall. You connected with me as a shy kid and gave me one place in the school where I felt I belonged.

College Years

WANDA BRACKETT: You believed in me, and I knew it.

STERLING BRACKETT: you put up with me, and I knew it. I knew you still liked me even though it was not easy!

DALE JENKINS AND DOUG JONES: You guys were upperclassmen. You treated me well and helped me belong.

DOROTHY JEAN FURLONG: I will never forget your lesson about how to walk with God. You took off your glasses, took a step forward, and said, "That is how you walk with God. And after you do that, you do it again."

Our Early Years in Mishawaka, Indiana

ED AND SHARON FARTHING: You guys served us, befriended us, and believed in us. It's hard to quantify the impact you had on my kids.

JEFF AND LAURA McWHIRT: You guys served us, befriended us, and believed in us. You gave us more than we would ever deserve.

DEAN AND JEAN RICE: You moved from a different state and served us with your lives. That is still humbling to think about.

ART MATZKVECH: You believed in us and gave us a chance to serve. You kept seeing our gift and helping us find a way to use it.

The Oklahoma Years

LINCOLN CHRISTIAN SCHOOL: We taught here for many years, and we met some amazing people. Our kids got to experience amazing teachers and coaches.

CHURCH ON THE MOVE: Hundreds of people from this church have made investments into our family. I cannot quantify your impact, and I cannot thank you enough.

CLINT PATTERSON: You taught me how to play fantasy football. Then you let me beat you at fantasy football. You made trades with me that always worked out in my favor. Mostly, you are a trail blazer, and you kept telling me to blaze a trail.

COREY MINTER: You looked at me and saw something I did not see. And you believed in me. And then you believed in me. And then you believed in me. And I know you still do.

JOEL WILAND: You are a puppy in human form. Your energy and bold love are unmatched.

JOHNIE HAMPTON: You wanted to hear what I had to say when I didn't think I had anything to say. And then you asked me to speak in front of other people. You elevated me when I didn't think I had anything of value to share.

RAY ADCOCK: When I first started out, I showed up at your business and stumbled through explaining what I do. You gave me a chance. You believed in me. You opened your heart to me.

ADAM AND SUE KENES: You decided to just keep showing up with us and for us. Walking through Sam's Club with you is still one of my favorite activities.

CHRIS COSTA: I got to sit at a table at a Denny's restaurant and listen to the simplest, yet the most profound message of the Gospel I have ever heard: "You're messed up, and there is nothing wrong with you." Chris, you move me.

KELLEN COWAN: You told me, "Don't stop doing what you are doing!" Every now and then, when I was losing courage, I would reach out to you. And you would tell me again, "Don't stop doing what you are doing!"

ALAN THOMAS: I came to you with my problem. You saw my gift, and you gave me a sword!

IFEANYI BELLAMY: You were there at the beginning. Your spirit is infectious. I always knew what you thought about me.

BRETT WILSON: You fully know me, yet you fully believe in me. You look past any deficiencies, and you see the gift in me. You empower me.

STEVE KATSIS: You are a giant of a man. Thanks for believing in us and standing shoulder to shoulder with us.

DARIEN GIBSON: You had the courage—and the love—to venture into the unknown with me. I'm not sure I will ever know how much that means.

KALEB AND MARISA WOOLEVER: You saw a next step for us to take when we didn't even see it ourselves. Thanks for using your gift in our lives.

BRETT RICHISON: Nobody asked you to support us. You just decided to support us.

CRAIG AND DAWN CHESSER: I don't even know what to say about the two of you. Thanks for being an example of boldness.

DAN MILLER AND THE EAGLES COMMUNITY: Dan, your life is inspiring. The community you have built is full of bold people who are pursuing bold lives together. The Tuesday-morning updraft group was an oasis for me. Building this business would have never happened without you.

THE TUESDAY NIGHT BOARD OF DIRECTORS: We cheer each other on to take bold steps. Thank you for being in my corner.

THE MONDAY MORNING DENNY'S DUDES (AND OUR WAITRESS, MISTY): Showing up and getting to be around you guys on Monday mornings encourages me to keep showing up everywhere else.

Endorsements

I have had a front-row seat as Mark walked through each step in his journey toward freedom. As his wife, his personal step into freedom is what opened the door for us to have an empowered marriage and share a powerful love I never knew was possible. As I read this book, I am so thankful he had the courage and the humility to take each of these steps. As you read this book, I hope you will embrace the hope for your own life and take your own step to freedom.

—*Adena*, Mark's wife

The ultimate life mentor isn't just someone that you want to learn what they know. You want to BE who they are. That is who my dad is to me. I've seen him in every kind of setting you can imagine, and I can tell you that there isn't a single thing he teaches that he isn't already boldly pursuing himself. He lives it out at home and in the world.

—*Matthew Delaney*, Mark's son

Some people live their whole life without ever being an active participant in it. This book will help you step into freedom and unlock your potential to live a truly fulfilling life. A life you can look back on and be proud of.

—*Kelsie Delaney*, Mark's daughter

I had the privilege of watching my dad enjoy the life change that resulted from freedom. It was like meeting him all over again! This book isn't just another book, it provides unique access to a life transformed and the simple clarifying perspectives that will help you take bold and exciting steps in your own life.

—*Andrew Delaney*, Mark's son

Mark is an amazing man who lives out what he teaches. Mark has been instrumental in helping me and others live a life full of purpose.

—*Layle Devilbiss*, friend

If you are satisfied with where you are in your life and want to continue living your version of the status quo, don't listen to Mark Delaney. But if you want to be challenged to live the life the Creator of the Universe intended for you to live—that version that feels a little scary, but you know deep down you could be living—then absorb every word in this book from Mark Delaney. (Full disclosure: You are likely to be challenged, stretched, and encouraged to step into a level of abundance you may have only dreamed of.) Mark is the real deal—congratulations on finding him. You should consider yourself blessed; I certainly do!

—ALAN THOMAS, mentor

Everyone needs to get a copy of Mark's book. There is so much passion behind the publication of these words. This book can restore marriages and families. It will bring hope, redemption, freedom, and purpose to your life. This book will help you live the life you were created to live.

—SHARON WRIGHT, sister

I have taken several courses and attended many groups led by Mark. He has helped me to see my life in a whole new way. He has helped me to live my life fulfilling my true purpose, and he has helped me let go of past mistakes that were holding me back.

—AMY BRESHEARS, friend

Mark is a man with a compelling message that invites you to take a bold step toward a deeper life of purpose. He has an eye for reducing the complex, and he draws from his many years of helping others and his own notable transformation journey. A master of the metaphor, through this book, Mark will help you till the soil of your life and live a life of boldness and authenticity!

—SCOTT TANG, friend

"An inspiring and captivating read. Mark not only shows you how to break free from self-limiting beliefs, but gives you a clear roadmap to embrace a life of bold authenticity. It's a game-changing read that will resonate with anyone seeking personal growth."

—DARIEN GIBSON, DarienGibson.com

Mark sincerely loves people and is passionate about helping them see their potential. He has the gift of simplifying complex topics and he uses this gift daily to help lead people to freedom. If you're interested in having powerful relationships and living purposefully, I highly recommend his content.

—NICK NELSON, Friend and Founder of Mission 15:4

CONTENTS

INTRODUCTION

My friend, I am writing this book with joyful desperation for you. I know what it's like to feel trapped outside of the life you want to live. I also know what it's like to leave that trap and live bold and free. In the pages to come, I will give you words, pictures, and action steps to help you find your freedom.

We all want freedom. But what is it? Am I living free? If I am not, what steered me off course? What is the pathway to a life of freedom? These are gutsy questions to ask. But they must be asked. All our lives carry a weight of significance. Because our lives matter so much, we must ask these questions.

The core of freedom is being able to live out the life for which you were made. Freedom is the ability to be comfortable in your own skin. We all have problems. We all have reasons to be insecure. We have all messed up. But one question matters: **Will I be the person I was made to be?** To me, this is what freedom feels like. It is living with the bold sense that I am being me. I don't have to pretend. I am living out the life I was made for. I don't feel trapped. I don't wake up to fix myself—because I wake up to be myself. I am boldly being me. That is freedom.

Without freedom, our dreams are covered over by our fears. Without freedom, anxiety prevents us from having peace. Without freedom, we protect our lives with so much effort that we stifle it. Without freedom, we try to force our lives to happen.

It's hard to define what freedom is, but it seems easy to describe life when you don't have it. Here is one simple question that will help you to gauge whether you are living in freedom: Are you hiding something about yourself? If so, you may not be living in freedom. But that's okay. This book will guide you through your journey to freedom.

I am writing because until the age of forty-seven, I was living my life in a cage. The cage was invisible, yet it was incredibly tangible to my heart and mind. In that cage, I felt like nothing but an overweight, underachieving man. Right outside that cage, I could see an image of the man I was made to be. I could see it every day. In my mind, I could see a cape hanging from a hook on the wall outside of my cage. I thought I needed to lose weight in order to go out and be that man. I was wrong. I needed freedom.

That cape haunted me. It represented a difference I was supposed to make. It represented the people who needed me to be who I was made to be. Inside my cage, I was comforted daily by oatmeal cream pies, potato chips, and biscuits. They were the reason I was in the cage, but they were also my best friends inside the cage. Every day I sat in that cage and ate my frustrations while staring at that cape. **Every day I told myself, _If I lose weight, I can get out and go be that person with a cape. And every day I failed._** I did not need to lose my problem. I needed to leave my problem. I needed to leave that cage. Only freedom could get me out of that cage.

I found freedom. And now I am sprinting through the wilderness of life and roaring with purpose. If you can imagine a lion wearing a cape, that is how I consistently feel every day. Now, my greatest joy is helping other people find freedom and purpose. My only burden is knowing that someone else is trapped outside the life they were made to live.

I am writing this book for people who feel like they were made for more, but who have a habit that is holding them back. **I know the feeling of living a life where the dreams of your heart are trapped by the habits of your life.** I know that pain. I can sense that frustration when I see it in others. And I will not sit on the sidelines and be a spectator of your pain.

For me, I see life as a giant wilderness. There are trees and bushes everywhere. The trees tell us to climb them to achieve success. But the higher you climb the trees, you only find smaller limbs—and they won't support you. There are also bushes everywhere that provide hiding places for the weary and broken. Those bushes grow up around us and become the cages in which we live. **I see you in that cage. I am not going to leave you in it. In this book, I am coming for you.** I will walk through thorny bushes and circle around brush fires to come for you. I want you out of that bush. The world needs you. Your life has a purpose. It is not too late for you to be who you were meant to be.

I need to ask you to rest as you read this book. Don't try to change. Don't try to fix yourself. Just know that I am racing through the brush to get to you. It's not too late. You are not too messed up.

 ## My Challenge for You

At the end of each chapter, I will give you a challenge. **Do yourself a favor and complete each challenge.** I will be your coach. I will be your guide. But nothing I say and nothing you read can replace the action steps that need to be taken.

> So, here is your first challenge: **Find someone to take on this journey with you.** Keep it simple. You don't have to tell them about the specific changes you are looking for. You can simply say, "I am looking for some change in my life. I'm not living out all that I am capable of living. I want to know if you are willing to take a journey of change with me."

Consider this to be a book study with action steps. Your plan with your teammate can be simple. Just read this book and complete the challenge that comes with each chapter.

CHAPTER 1

There Is Hope

Maybe you have been stuck in a cage for a long time. Maybe you've been there your whole life. That does not scare me. That does not concern me one bit. I am racing toward that bush in which you find yourself. I will help pull the vines off you. You may have had a problem for thirty years. You may have lost all sight of what you were made for. Sit tight, my friend. I am coming for you. If you see a lion wearing a cape, don't be afraid—that's just me. I'm just a common man, but I have a bold message for you. Like I shared earlier, *When common people take uncommon steps with other common people, miracles become common.* Our lives have much in common. Together we will take uncommon steps. I am believing that miracles will happen when we do this.

Can I tell you a couple of stories? A young man emailed me several years ago. I want you to read portions of what he wrote.

Mark, I've been wanting to reach out to you for quite a while now. I've just been too embarrassed and prideful to actually do so. If it's at all possible, I could really use your help. Ever since I graduated from high school, things have just snowballed one on top of another to the point of where I'm at now. I don't like the person I am when I look in the mirror. I don't feel like I'm 'me' anymore... and when I see glimpses of who I once was, or when I have moments of clarity, it takes me by surprise, because I miss that version of me.

In 2016, I started viewing and searching for pornography. Despite my numerous attempts of going to counseling and seeing numerous counselors, having accountability partners and groups, and using software tools to block the images, the problem has only gotten worse. I began fighting depression in 2016 as well. In 2018, I started having suicidal thoughts, began taking medication for depression, and had to go on medical leave from school that following semester.

In January and February, I was not doing very good at all. I was so depressed, and I didn't have a roommate, which was the perfect storm for isolation and attempts to numb the pain through food, Netflix, and pornography. I didn't even know if I was going to be able to graduate. But after a conversation with my parents, I mustered up enough fight to push on and do whatever possible to graduate.

I tried my best to have a hopeful outlook on the future. But anytime someone asked me about what I was going to do next, I began to shut down. I felt like I was having an anxiety attack anytime someone asked me about what I was going to do. A friend, that I love like a brother, reached out to me. Twice actually. But I began feeling so full of shame and felt so embarrassed of who I had become that I didn't respond to him. I finished school, came back home, and became this anxious, depressed, gluttonous, pride-filled couch potato with no hope.

I want to find joy in the little things. To be grateful for what I have and who I'm with for this season. I want to get to a point where I feel like I could truly pursue a godly woman. Have a family. Be a godly husband and father.

I've just been very embarrassed about where I'm at and who I've become, and I haven't wanted to share that with anyone. I don't want to hide anymore. And I don't want others to feel like they have to hide either.

I immediately responded to "Thomas" (not his real name), and we started meeting together. At our first meeting, I told him, "We are not going to talk about your addictions, or your depression, or your suicidal thoughts. We are going to talk about your purpose." We met in a restaurant regularly for five weeks. I drew him pictures of the forest. I helped him see how he had gotten where he was, and how he could get back to the life he was made to live.

He showed up each week and kept taking the practical action steps. Because of those steps, he was able to leave that bush in which he had been stuck. Within six weeks, he had applied for a job out of state, received the position, and was packing his bags. I spoke with him a few months ago, and he told me about the person he has been dating and to whom he is about to propose. Freedom enabled this to happen. This is the journey I want to take you on as well.

Here is another story—this time, about a young mom.

> One woman was so down about her life that she was not getting out of bed. She had a husband and young kids at home who were watching her lie in bed most of the day. She was stuck in her life. She met with my wife and went through "The Purpose Mastermind." (I'll explain this later.) After two weeks, her husband asked what was happening. He was pleasantly surprised at the change in her behavior. She was out of bed early in the morning, and she was aggressively living life. My wife, Adena, did not talk to her about her problems. She did not ask, "Why do you lie around all day?" She did not talk about how she was letting other people down. Instead, Adena talked about her purpose. Within a month or two, this woman was boldly pursuing what her life was made to be.

Here is another story—about a couple who was married for over twenty years.

> A couple came to us who had been married for over twenty years. They had been high school sweethearts. They are both great people. But they are no longer great with each other. Twelve years ago, their marriage turned in the wrong direction. Hope was gone. Romance was gone. Belief was gone.

We had a conversation with them and said, "We can help you. But we are not going to talk about your marriage." We said to the husband, "One thing matters: Will you be the person you were made to be?" And we asked the wife, "Will you be the person you were made to be?" When trouble hits in our lives, it changes us. But as we focus on the trouble, we neglect to see what we have become as a person. We met with this couple and walked them through "The Purpose Mastermind." We guided them to be the people they were made to be. That changed their marriage. That restored hope and belief. But this did not just impact their marriage—it made them better for everyone in their lives.

One last story.

A thirty-two-year-old man came to me and said, "I don't know how I got here..." Over the past year, he had started to struggle with an alcohol problem. Everyone was concerned. So was he. His wife didn't know what to do, and it threatened their marriage and their family, including their two small children. I did not talk to him about alcohol. I talked to him about his purpose. I showed him how he got into this trap, but we did not focus on what he did inside of the trap. He, and the people in his life, were thinking that his habit needed to change. But his habit was not his problem. It was just the result of his problem. He could have spent the next thirty years of his life going through addiction programs. His wife and friends could have spent their entire lives focusing on his habit. What he needed was to get out of the trap. When he left the trap and started pursuing his purpose, then he left his drinking problem.

I don't know what has caused you to become stuck. I don't know the habit or behavior pattern that has you feeling like you are trapped outside the life you dream of living. You will see in this journey that the story of all our lives is really quite similar. I'll be bold and say this: I am not afraid of the problem you have. I am not concerned with how long you have had it. I just want you to have your freedom.

Can I be really bold? I think I know what is wrong with you. Do you want me to tell you? Are you ready for it? I know what is wrong with you. Go to this QR code and I will tell you face-to-face what is wrong with you.

I know what's wrong with you.
#1

Scan the QR code for more

This book is not about your problem—it is all about your freedom. It is not the study of what happened to you. It is not the study of how you messed up. It is about the journey to freedom and being all that you were made to be.

As we prepare to begin, I want to let you know what to expect on this journey.

- I want you to understand how you got to where you are.

- I want you to understand the one step to freedom.

- I want you to understand how to walk out that life of freedom.

In each chapter, you will see pictures. I will tell you how my story looks in the picture, and then I'll share principles to help you understand how it applies to your journey.

 My Challenge for You

Find someone in your life who has inspired you because they made some type of change in their life. Maybe they lost weight or overcame an addiction. Maybe they overcame an obstacle in their life. Talk to that person and ask about their journey. Ask them how they did what they did. Your goal is not to get advice on your specific problem. Just take in their story.

CHAPTER 2

What Do You Really Want?

Let's pretend we are sitting in a room full of one hundred people of various ages. We will ask them this one question: What do you want from life? After we get past the superficial answers about bigger houses, boats, and six-pack abs, we will get to the big things we all truly want. What are those big things? If I were asked, I would say they are purpose, freedom, and love. At the end of this chapter, I will ask you to spend some time thinking about what you really want.

My Story

From the youngest of ages, I loved to help people. One of my favorite ways of showing up in life was by making choco-late-chip cookies for others. I gave them to my paper-route customers, I took them to church, and I took them to work. I suppose that simple action represented what I wanted to be for people. I wanted to do something to help them feel loved.

I think my favorite memories of childhood were the simple ones that involved just experiencing life with people—especially when it involved doing meaningful things. I remember going Christmas shopping with my sister. I remember helping my older brother memorize the toppings for the sandwiches at the fast-food restaurant where he had just started working.

There is one moment I think perfectly illustrates how I felt about life in the purest of forms. I remember getting out of the bathtub as a little boy and getting an idea about my towel. I put it around my neck like a cape. It felt magical! Nobody had to tell me to do that. That moment is a picture of the life I wanted to live. At five years old, I had done nothing but make noises and make messes. I had no muscles, and I had no talent. But inside of me there was a heart to be a common hero. I wanted my life to make a difference.

Your Story

What is *your* story? Think back to when you were young. Hopefully there was a time in your life when things were simple enough for you to have an innocence about who you were. What made you feel alive? I have spoken to some people who feel their childhoods robbed them of ever living with a sense of freedom and innocence.

I believe this happens to all of us at some point. It's the human experience. For some people, it happens at the youngest of ages. For others, it occurs in high school or after college. It can happen in middle age. But at some point, life brings us to some deep introspection. When problems become big in our life, they scream out for our attention. But maybe the problems are just the result of a deeper problem of purposelessness. **If an empty life is causing problems, what is more important: fixing the problem or fixing the emptiness?**

I recall a man telling me that when he thought back to the early years of his life, he thought life was just love. That it was just about living and receiving love. That is what he believed until his parents became abusive. Then his perspective changed.

I was talking with some men in a prison, and I asked them, "What did you want from life when you were a kid?" Several of them responded by saying, "Survival. That is all that I remember wanting. I never recall dreaming about good things."

When we study our lives, we tend to look back and think about what went wrong. But I want to challenge you to look back to the innocence of your childhood and remember what your heart wanted to experience in life.

 ## My Challenge for You

> What do you want from life? What brings joy to your heart? What makes your eyes spark with life? Take the time to answer that question. Write down your thoughts. Writing down your ideas and thoughts can help you put into words what you are wrestling with. If you are on this journey with someone else, have that discussion together.

CHAPTER 3

What Went Wrong? How Did I Respond?

We all want our lives to be about big, fulfilling things. For me, the big things are purpose, freedom, and love. If I am living out those three things, then I have everything. The storyline of each of our lives is really quite similar. Notice the picture. We embark on our journeys with the idea that we are good, that we will do something good in life, and that we will experience good things in life. But somewhere along the path, something goes wrong. Either something goes wrong because of us or something bad happens to us.

When this happens, we leave this path, and we go into a bush. We end up living very differently in that bush because we see our lives very differently. We may not see ourselves as good anymore. We may not think we can do good. We may think that a good life isn't possible anymore. We may have also lost our trust in other people.

My Story

I recall a story from about third grade. I was in class minding my own business. I was on my path. But then the teacher told the class to line up to go to the nurse's office. We were lined up on one side of the hallway and then called over one at a time to have our height and weight checked. One person called out the numbers while another adult wrote them down. I was a chunky kid, and so my number was higher than that of the other kids. The other kids made comments about my weight, and I did not know how to respond. **I might have gone to school thinking about a good life, but I went home thinking about my weight. I left my path.**

When I was about ten years old, I rode my bike across the neighborhood to play tackle football with some friends. That was a thrilling thing for me. I was on my path. It was great—until some other kid pushed my face into the ground after tackling me. How did I respond? I immediately got on my bike and rode back toward my home. But I did not make it all the way home, because across the street from my house was a park. I rode to the back of that park and hid in the bushes. **I did not know what to think about what had happened. So, I left my path.**

When I was in sixth grade, I tried out to join the band. I was excited at the opportunity to play an instrument at school. I was on my path. The band teacher asked me what I wanted to play, and I told him I wanted to play the trumpet. He handed it to me and asked me to make a noise with it. He looked at me and said something innocently, but it stunned me. He said, "Your lips are too big." **I did not know how to respond to that.** So, for the rest of my childhood, I was self-conscious about the size of my lips. **I left my path.**

When I was an adult, I started to gain a lot of weight. I was desperate to live a life that mattered and make a difference, but all I saw in the mirror was an overweight man who could not make a difference. All the failings of my life sent me to the pantry or refrigerator. There was not any specific major thing that went wrong. I was overweight, and that was enough for me to think of myself as a loser. **I saw my problem, and I left my path.**

My response to my problem was worse than my problem. Here were my responses:

1. I hated myself. My problem was my identity. Being overweight is an awful identity.

2. I was bitter at other people for judging me and my problem. I did this with or without people judging me. There were a small number of times when I felt people actually judged me, but I lived as if the whole world judged me all the time.

3. I avoided the problem. For me, this meant avoiding the bathroom scale. I just pretended the problem didn't exist. As long as I didn't step on the scale, I didn't have a problem.

4. I decided I had been born this way, and I didn't need to see being overweight as a problem. I decided the standard of weight was completely wrong. I protested the charts at the doctor's office that showed the levels of healthy weight.

These four responses did not help at all. They were instinctual responses, but they did not serve me or solve the problem. They took me further away from what I really needed.

Your Story

Earlier I mentioned a man who thought that life would just be about love. However, when he was a little boy, his parents started to abuse him. From that moment on, he left his path. He said, "For the first five years, life was just about love. After my parents started abusing me, I became a different person. I lived by the motto that 'I am going to hurt you before you hurt me'." **He left his path.**

A young man wanted to live a life that he could be proud of. But his dad was never proud of him, so he took nothing seriously in life. **He left his path.**

A young girl was molested at a young age. She used to like herself, but after that happened, she changed. She became so unsure of herself that she began to stutter severely. **She left her path.**

A teenage boy was confident in who he was until he started watching pornography. Now he hates himself. **He left his path.**

A man wants to make a difference with his life, but then he causes an accident, and someone is hurt. He no longer believes he is worthy of making a difference with his life. **He left his path.**

The stories could go on and on. But the storyline is the same. Each of us is excited about our lives—until something goes wrong, and then we leave the path. That path represents a way of thinking about our lives. On that path, we are dreaming of purpose, freedom, and love. After the negative event, we leave that path and are no longer dreaming of these things.

 ## My Challenge for You

Here is my challenge for you for this chapter. Think of examples from your life in which something went wrong. How did you respond? How did it change you? If you are on this journey with someone else, this would make for a great conversation. *You do not need to analyze the event. Focus more on observing your response to the event.*

CHAPTER 4

Why Did I Leave the Path?

In the last chapter, we shared stories of how we have responded to the negative events in our lives. In short, we may be living our lives on that path of purpose, freedom, and love, but then something goes wrong, and we leave that path. But why? **The answer to this is paramount, because if I realize why I left the path, I will have a clue about how to get back on the path.**

Human instinct says *the event* is why we left that path. Certainly, that is part of the equation. The events that happen in people's lives can be extremely painful and impacting. You will notice in the examples I gave in the last chapter that the pattern is the same for almost everyone. The storyline is the same. Notice the pattern in the picture.

1. I am living the life I want to live.

2. Something bad happens.

3. I begin to live a different life.

But why? Why did we leave that path? Do we live the rest of our lives saying, "My life could have been great, but something bad happened, so my life cannot be great"? Do we spend the rest of our lives saying, "I wanted to make a difference, but my mistake has disqualified me"? We can all agree that bad things have happened in our lives. It's part of the human experience, and it cannot be escaped. We have all caused harm in some way, and we have all been harmed in some way.

Many people allow these negative events to knock them off their paths for the rest of their lives. The event shapes the rest of their existence. Does it have to be that way? No. I declare a resounding *no*!

I have sympathy for the pain people have experienced. But people need more than sympathy for their lives. What they really need is to have freedom. I would rather people get back to the path they were made for instead of living the rest of their lives compensating for something that went wrong. **Blaming the event for the result of our life will not move us forward.**

The following question must be answered correctly, because it is a key component to regaining our freedom: **Why did I leave the path?** It was my response to what happened. My human pride gave me a false pathway to save myself. To be honest, I naturally blame the event for making me leave the path, but that answer doesn't solve anything. If I believe the event sent me off the path, then it is what has the power to keep me off the path.

So, why did we leave the path? Simply put, our human instinct was to save ourselves. That is why we left the path.

My Story

Should I blame the band teacher for telling me that my lips were too big? Do I spend the rest of my life protesting trumpet manufacturers for making their mouthpieces too small? The truth is much more relevant.

WHAT'S THE REAL PROBLEM?

"STUPID MOUTHPIECE"   "I WONDER WHAT THEY THINK OF MY LIPS?"   "BAND DIRECTORS ARE MEAN!"

Can I tell you why this event was so impactful in my life? I was afraid of what people thought about how I looked. That is why I was so impacted. I was not capable of handling what others thought about how I looked. What was my bigger life problem? What the band teacher said, or what I thought about myself? The comment by the band teacher did not cause me to live in fear of what people thought about how I looked. The comment by the band teacher *revealed that I already had that fear*.

I told the story of when a kid pushed my face into the ground. There is no doubt that he drove my face into the ground, but I am the one who drove my bicycle into the bush to hide. **My instinctual response to save myself was my bigger problem.**

Much of the story of my life revolves around me becoming overweight. My response to this problem *was* the problem. My instinct to save myself caused me to never talk about it with anyone else. My pride kept me hiding my problem. And in hiding my problem, I was missing the actual answer.

Your Story

Why did you leave the path? I am not trying to say that we are to blame for leaving the path, but we did play a role. This is actually good news. Later you will see how there is a role we can play in order to get back onto the path.

How did you respond to the events of your life? Examine what was really going on inside of you under the surface. Maybe you were afraid of what people thought of you. Maybe you were afraid of anything being wrong with you. Maybe pride caused you to be afraid of ever messing up. Maybe you were afraid that what someone did to you would forever damage you. This could have caused you to put up walls to protect yourself from more damage being done to you.

My Challenge for You

Think about the life-altering situations you have faced. Examine your response. What does your response say about you? This conversation is about your freedom, so think about this from the perspective of becoming free. This does not mean you are to blame for what happened, and we are not trying to understand the actual event that happened. We are working to understand *our own response* to the event that took place. Take some time and journal about the situations that shaped your life. Reflect on your responses.

CHAPTER 5

What Happens in the Bush?

Life in the bush is far different than life on the path of purpose, freedom, and love. We went into the bush because it looked like a way of escape. As we talked about in chapter 4, the bush gives us a way to save ourselves. When something goes wrong, our human instinct sounds like this:

- "Nobody can know what happened to me!"

- "Nobody can know what I did!"

- "I have to make sure this never happens again!"

- "I need to protect myself!"

The bush is advertised as a place of protection for me. It's an immediate answer to my problem. It makes complete sense to my human instinct to jump into that bush. The sign on the bush says, QUICK—THIS WAY! YOU CAN PROTECT YOURSELF HERE! But the sign doesn't come with any warnings. It doesn't tell you what will happen once you enter.

Although there is an initial comfort in hiding, it does not take long before a far greater threat begins to loom over our lives. This life in hiding is far different than the life we were intended to live.

In the bush, I am not just hiding my problem. I am hiding my gift. I am hiding my love. **I have exchanged a focus on my future for a focus on hiding from my past.** I am barricading myself from my future. Think of a bush and consider what life is like there.

- The visibility is very limited. We become deceived. We do not realize that we are looking at everything through a veil of branches.

- People have a hard time seeing us. We think we have hidden our problem from others, but in reality, we look confusing to people. They have to try to figure out who we are through those branches.

- The lack of visibility represents our inability to have vision. It is very difficult to dream of what your life can be while you are hiding within the bush.

- The bush becomes a barricade that prevents us from experiencing others. We can't hug someone through a bush.

- The bush blocks others from getting close to us. The bush proclaims itself as protection, but in reality, living disconnected from others is far from what we really want, and it exposes us to the dangers of isolation.

- The bush makes sure that anything good that could happen between us and other people becomes very difficult—almost impossible. We went into the bush to block the possibility of anyone hurting us. But we have also blocked the possibility of giving and receiving great love.

- In the bush, it seems that nobody can hurt us. While we try to prevent someone from hurting us, we lose the ability to see how we hurt others.

We would like to think the bush just hides our problem, our failures, our mistakes, etc. But when we step into the bush, we also hide our gifts. Our love. Our purpose. We mistakenly think we are going on as normal. We believe the lie that nothing else is impacted. We just hid this one "thing." But everything is impacted. Every relationship has to suffer with the addition of the bush. Every relationship that matters has to weave its way through the awkward branches that surround us. Everyone feels it. They may be trying to love us, but it is awkward. They don't know why, but it's not easy to love this different person we have become. *We* become difficult to deal with. **Simply put, the bush distorts how you see people, and it distorts how people see you.**

It's important that I bring up what I call a *false freedom*. This is what happens when I think the "bush" version of me is actually right for me. Instead of saying, "I am living a distorted life," it is easier to proclaim, "There is nothing wrong with me! This is who I am supposed to be." This would be like me saying, "There is nothing wrong with weighing 350 pounds. The doctors are wrong. The culture is wrong. Weighing what I weigh is fine. I was born to weigh this much." This would be a "false freedom." I would love to change the standards to make them fit my reality, but this would be a false freedom. A false freedom says that nothing is wrong with me, and I'm perfect as I am. Real freedom is to be honest about who I really am.

The worst kind of freedom is what I call a *fancy freedom*. This is when you have the ability to dress up your life and make it look like everything is all just fine. A person with "fancy freedom" lives in a bush but has the ability to dress up that bush and make it look great. It does not matter how much you dress up the bush for people; it will have the same results. I'll give some examples. This is a person who has a leadership position that gives him a good image in front of others. He can use this as a cover-up for who he really is inside that bush. This fancy freedom could also be a person who lives in a mansion. Great wealth can enable us to purchase a monthly dose of fancy freedom. We can use our wealth to make our life appear to be perfect, but underneath the designer clothes, we wear inmate clothes.

Fancy freedom takes place when we can portray an image of freedom to others. But this is not freedom at all. I have met people who use their good looks to project this fancy freedom. Some men will use bodybuilding to project a false sense of freedom to the world. Wealth, good looks, and bodybuilding are not bad things. But if they are used to cover up our bondage, they are dangerous. **Ultimately, fancy freedom is fake freedom.** We become actors. And acting is exhausting. When freedom is fake, it is frustrating instead of liberating.

Fancy, fake freedom traps people in the life they built. Nobody can point out your bondage because you think you have no bondage. I'll give an example. For many people, bush living shows up with an ugly behavior. Anger, drinking, overeating, binging on the phone, etc. Other people in the bush will live with an insatiable appetite for creating great wealth. This does not appear to be a problem. It even gets applauded by some. The reality is that some people use work as a coping mechanism. Their pursuit of generational wealth might be destroying them as much as the person who is pursuing the next bottle of alcohol.

I understand false, fancy freedom. I used it for a long time. I was able to be in leadership positions that made me appear to be doing great. I was not a fraud. I was just not free. I stayed away from the taboo topic of food, and I made sure the people close to me didn't bring it up, either. I kept working to project an image to people of who I was. I had a fake freedom. Those people who were close to me were forced to live with the consequences of my fake freedom.

My Story

I was working hard to hide being overweight. My biggest decision every day was to find a shirt that fit loosely. As long as my shirt was loose, I was fine. At least that is what I told myself. I had two basic thoughts that took up way too much time in my mind: *What do people think about how I look?* And, *when can I eat again?*

I saw myself as a failure. My failure was attached to me. I wanted to hide it in that bush from people, but it just made me become consumed with dwelling on my problem. My problem and my identity were intertwined. I did not have dreams of what I could be. I only had nightmares of who I was.

If I walked into a room, my first thought was, *What do they think about what I look like?* The thought was the same if I met a new person. I thought everyone looked at me and judged me by how I looked. I did not think about *them*. I wondered what *they* thought about how I looked.

Your Story

I'll give an example of how this plays out in a marriage. A common scenario looks like this. Two people get married, and they are excited about each other. Things are great until she sees pornography on his phone. She confronts him, and they both go into a bush. He is ashamed of himself. He doesn't think about her the same way. Instead of being excited about her, he wonders if she is still thinking about what he did. She goes into a bush for a different reason. She is hurt. She looks at him differently. She is wondering what he is thinking and doing and how she can make sure his behavior changes. Her instinct is to protect herself and change her husband.

This couple sees themselves differently, and they see each other differently. The problem was painful for her, and it was shameful for him. The problem mattered, but their response to the problem determines if they will live the rest of their lives in that bush because of the problem. **In the bush, we create a different way of thinking. That new thinking will keep us stuck in the problem.**

This chapter began with one question: What happens in the bush? In short, we become a different person in the bush. We become someone who is dominated by instincts that prevent us from becoming who we really want to be.

This journey is not about studying the event that happened. It is about understanding why the situation derailed us—and learning how we can get back to the life we were made to live. We can leave the bush. And when we do, we step into freedom.

 My Challenge for You

It is hard to do this kind of introspection. *But your life is worth it.* I want to challenge you to spend some time answering these questions: Do you feel like you are living in that bush? Do you think you are living the life that you were made to live? Are you living to protect yourself or to just be yourself? Are you more focused on hiding your mistakes or on sharing your gifts? In what ways are you living a "fancy freedom"?

CHAPTER 6

Why Does Bush Living Lead to Coping?

This question—"Why do we cope?"—must be answered. The answer to this question was life-changing for me. The common thought is that we are coping because of what happened to us. Or we are coping because of what we did wrong. But what if the answer is far different than that?

Let's go back to my childhood to illustrate. Remember the story about what the band leader said about my lips? Think of a little boy who strolls down the road to school and thinks something like this: *We have recess today! I hope we play kickball. I love playing kickball. Maybe I will be a team captain.* Later, that little boy is told that his lips are too big—and now his thinking changes. After that day, he walks to school with a mindset that says, *I hope nobody says anything about my lips today. Other people might notice and start picking on me. I wish my lips weren't so big.* Notice the drastic change in his outlook. One way of thinking causes him to step boldly into the day. But the thinking in the bush leads to deflated thinking that constantly says, "Your life is messed up. You messed up. Someone messed you up. You just stay behind that bush. You don't get to dream.

You don't get to matter. You don't get to have expectations anymore. Just hide." **Our dreams are replaced with a nightmare. Our hope is replaced with insecurity. Our purpose is replaced with a problem. Our excitement is replaced with anxiety. Simply put, when I went into hiding, I exchanged a life of purpose and meaning for a life in hiding.**

We don't realize this when the exchange first happens. We are just relieved to find a place of rescue. Think about this. How painful is it to go from thinking, *I'm a bright light in the world,* to *I'm a blight to the world.* Or the thought of *I have a life worth living* is exchanged with *I have a life that's only worth hiding.*

I think we are all born with the belief that "life is good" and "there is something good for me to be in this world. There is something important for me to do." **The greatest threat to our lives is not that something will go wrong. The greatest threat to our lives is that our lives will not become what they were made to be.** That may be the ultimate life pain.

In the bush, we are forced to cope. We cope because of the pain we want to numb. The pain is that our lives are no longer about purpose and chasing our dreams. What we cope with helps us to numb that awful pain. It distracts us from thoughts we do not want to have. So, our coping mechanism keeps drawing us back for more. We become trapped. **But we are not trapped by our problems. We are trapped by how we think about our problems.**

I summarize by saying this: **We cope because we have lost the life we were made to live.** What if we could get our life back? Maybe we wouldn't need to cope!

My Story

Any person who goes into the bush will have to cope. Consider this: **I have never heard a human speak these words**: "The only thing I wanted in life was to make a difference. I now realize I never will. But I'm okay with that." No human will ever honestly speak those words. There is too much pain to be felt when we settle for less than what our heart dreams of. That's why the only way to hide in the bush is to cope in the bush. For me, the bush became a prison. It was hard to even think of the possibilities of my life. I was too busy being distracted by this constant cycle:

- Any type of negative feeling or negative thing that happens...
  - > Eat food to feel better...

- Feel guilty for being overweight and eating too much...
  - > Eat more to feel better about eating too much...

- Feel bad about being an underachiever and letting people down...
  - > Eat more to get rid of the bad feeling...

- Repeat daily!

I hated that I was overweight. And every second I had to drag around the reminder. When I sat down, when I got up, when I tied my shoes, when I walked—everything I did, I was reminded of my weight. You get the idea. For each of us, our problems become a heavy weight that we carry around everywhere we go. We hate the problem. We get distracted by the problem. But the greatest pain is that we are not being who we were made to be.

Your Story

Personally, I believe that the people who are coping the most are the people who care the most. Maybe inside of you is a big heart to love people, but you feel like your relationships are all broken. The disappointment of that can cause you to turn to a coping mechanism to numb that pain. Maybe you have a big desire to be a person of impact, but you feel like you are just going through the motions. You find yourself drinking more and more. Maybe drinking is just a way to numb the pain because your life is not giving you the real substance you were made for.

We have all wandered into the bush at some point. Let's be honest: C: Coping is easier than facing the reality of our life. When we end up off the path, it feels like we are so lost in the wilderness that we have no way back. The point of this chapter is simple: I want you to think about why you're coping. I don't want you to stop coping. Ultimately, I want to help you alleviate the need to cope. I want the actual pain of your life to be alleviated. I want you to get back to your path of purpose, freedom, and love.

I'll challenge you with a few questions: Does it really matter what happened in your life that caused you to go into a bush and hide? If there is a way to be free, does it really matter why you were in prison to begin with? Does it really matter how you are coping? What if you quench the pain instead?

You don't need to stop coping right now. But I challenge you to be honest about how you cope. It may be a substance that you turn to. It may be an activity or a tactic you use with other people, like trying to control them. If you hide how you cope from others, you will also hide from yourself the real reason you cope.

My Challenge for You

Go have a conversation with someone and admit to them how you cope. And tell them why you are coping. If you need some help, start with this: "Can I tell you something? I (insert your coping mechanism) a lot. I do this more than I should." Once you do that, can you go one step further? Tell them why you turn to that coping mechanism. You could start with this: "I think I do this because I _____." (If you haven't figured out this answer yet, that is okay.)

CHAPTER 7

What Is the False Way of Escape?

The bush becomes a prison. And our coping mechanism is our cellmate. Every now and then, we look at the prison bars and make an attempt to get out. But it doesn't work. The most difficult prison to escape from is the one with invisible bars. And that is the prison that threatens us all. The invisible prison exists when we feel trapped outside of the life we were made to live. Our house may look great. Our job may be impressive. The external qualities of our life may appear to be fine, but at the same time our heart can feel trapped.

Recently I was meeting with some inmates in a prison in our community. They were in a program that helps inmates prepare for the day when they leave incarceration. When I visit them, I sense a real freedom in the room. These guys live in a physical prison, yet they live with a real sense of personal freedom. I asked them a strange question one day: "Why are you guys so free?" This story is better communicated through video, so use this QR code to hear how they responded to my question.

Why are you guys so free?
#2

*Scan the
QR code
for more*

I share this story with you to give you hope of escaping your own prison. If men who are in a physical prison can live free, can you live free in spite of what has gone wrong in your life? Yes, you can. You may feel like you are living in an invisible prison. Or you may be like I was and have an obvious physical problem that has become your prison. In the next chapter, I will talk about the one step to freedom. But first, it is important that you understand the lies that cause you to try the wrong way of escape.

Here are the common lies we encounter in the bush, and the truths we can think instead.

1. Here is the lie: *I have to fix my behavior in order to be free.*
   Here is the truth: *I cannot change my behavior until I am free.*

2. The lie: *My coping mechanism doesn't impact me in any other way.*
   The truth: *My coping mechanism impacts every area of my life.*

3. The lie: *I got myself into this mess, and I have to get myself out of this mess.*
   The truth: *Everything about my problem and my freedom involves others.*

4. The lie: *I am not supposed to have this problem, so I can't let anyone know.*
   The truth: *All humans have problems. I am not the only one, and others can relate.*

5. The lie: *If I fix up this bush, I can make it a pretty good place to live.*
   The truth: *The bush is barricading me from the life I really want.*

6. The lie: *Other people won't be hurt by me if I stay in this bush.*
   The truth: *If I stay in the bush, I am unable to see how I am hurting other people.*

7. The lie: *I am the only person living in a bush.*
   The truth: *Everyone lives in a bush at some point.*

8. The lie: *Hiding is protecting me.*
   The truth: *Hiding is hurting me.*

Each of these lies sounds right. They help us stay in the bush. They lead us to try the wrong way. This causes great frustration. It makes the prison bars stronger. It lengthens our prison sentence.

My Story

In my prison, I was either coping or planning an escape. Mostly coping. In my mind, I had etched an escape plan into the prison wall. I believed these lies, and it caused my escape plan to be wrong. My plan seemed so right, but it was upside down.

This was my escape plan:

- Step One: Lose weight.

- Step Two: Get freedom.

- Step Three: Come out of hiding.

Here is the escape plan that actually worked in my life:

- Step One: Come out of hiding.

- Step Two: Become free.

- Step Three: Go live my purpose (which caused me to lose weight).

As you think about my life, you might be wondering, *How much weight did he lose?* I would wonder the same thing. My highest was about 380, and my lowest was 282. Right now, I am 299. The shift in my mindset helped me to lose weight. Although I am not skinny yet, my focus is on losing the weight in my thinking so I can have the mindset I need for every part of my life.

However, don't miss the big thing. The *really* big thing. Since I left that prison of my life, I have been living bold and free. My life has become alive like it never was before. I know you want me to be skinny. And I wouldn't mind that, either. But I was made to be free. And the size of my body does not determine my freedom. That was a lie told to me in the bush. I spent enough years thinking, *Until I am skinny, I cannot be me.* That was a lie. A complete lie.

When people tell me I am looking really good, I am not sure how to respond. **Losing the weight on my body does not compare to gaining a life of freedom.** The great result of leaving the bush is not the removal of a problem. The great result of leaving the bush is the gaining of your life.

That is why I am writing this book. I want you to live your best, bold life. You must leave that bush in order to live that life. But you must first know the escape plan.

Your Story

My friend, you must be careful with these lies. The lie is often parked right next to the truth, so it can sound correct. But we can only park on the truth or park on the lie. If you park on the lie, then you miss the truth. Believing the lie prevents us from seeing the truth. That makes us try to solve our problem in a way that seems right, but it only makes things worse.

I have spoken with people who have spent thirty years trying to change a behavior problem. They have invested thousands of dollars trying different types of therapies. With every type of therapy, the goal was the same: to fix the problem. But it did not work. But what if this was the wrong goal to begin with? **What if focusing on our problem actually strengthens the prison bars and makes the problem bigger?**

When we work with people, we tell them from the start, "We are not going to talk about your problem." They may be struggling with addiction, depression, or marriage problems, but we are not going to focus on any of those things.

You do not need behavior change. You need freedom. And freedom changes your perspective. **It is not our problem that needs to change. How we think about our problem is what needs to change.**

 ## My Challenge for You

Look over the lies that were listed in this chapter and identify which ones you believe. Be honest about any lie you actually believe to be true. Then, have a conversation with someone about the lies you have believed. Talk about why you believed the lie.

CHAPTER 8

What Is the One Step to Freedom?

The journey of the first part of this book brings us to this one question: What is the one step to freedom? **Come out of hiding.** That is it. Step out of hiding. Notice the picture. It was one bold step that we took that caused us to end up in the bush. Every fiber of our being took us into that bush. Our human instinct used the bush to save us from our troubles. Now I am telling you to do the opposite of your human instinct. **I am challenging you to do the opposite of what you originally did to save yourself.**

This step I am challenging you to take is very simple. But it's incredibly awkward. Nothing in your common reasoning will want to take this step. You will have to fight off any of the lies listed in chapter 7 to take this step. The step into that bush was a bold effort to save yourself and control the results of your life. The step I am talking about is the opposite of that. I am compelling you to do the opposite of what you thought rescued you. You may need to let go of what you are doing to control the situation of your life.

As you read this, you might be wondering, *How will that help me fix my problem?* If you are asking that question, do you believe lie #1 from chapter 7? **If you are asking that question, it demonstrates that you are not stuck in your problem. You are stuck in how you think about your problem.** What if, instead, you said, *What have I got to lose? Nothing else has helped me.* I would like to gently, yet boldly, put my hand on your back and nudge you forward. Take the one step to freedom. Step out of hiding.

My Story

For most of my life, I was trapped. I was consumed with how I looked. I thought my body was embarrassing. I worked hard to find clothes that would hang loosely on my body. I worked very hard to hide my problem and build a reputation in spite of how I looked. It was exhausting. I only needed to do one thing to step into freedom: **Come out of hiding**. Metaphorically speaking, all I needed to do was take off my shirt. I just needed to stop hiding my problem.

I know that sounds simple. But admitting my problem was completely opposite of what I spent my life trying to do. **I thought that the admission of my problem would disqualify me.** I had no choice but to cover up my problem so I could at least hope that other people thought well of me. As I write these words, I shiver as I think of the man I used to be. I think of how limiting it was to live that way. I could never go back to that way of thinking. I have tasted freedom, and I will not go back.

Every day I spent trying to cover up my problem made it more difficult to admit it to others. I guess I was a pretty stubborn person. The more I worked to protect my reputation, the bigger the prison walls became.

If I had not come to a desperate place in life, I'm not sure I would have ever come out of hiding. I was not desperate to be skinny. I was desperate to make a difference. I was desperate to be free. **That is why I feel sorry for anyone who is able to decorate their bush and make it look good. It enables them to keep living a fake life at the expense of living a real life...a free life.**

That was my story for a long time. Looking back, I think people saw me as a good man. I held respectable positions in leadership. I could use my career as a way of boosting my reputation. I didn't think much of myself as a man other than the jobs I held. But this was trapping me. My work became a source of identity for me. I could point people to that, and hopefully they would think highly of me.

I felt like my life was trapped in a cage in two different ways. On the one hand, I was living with a physical problem that was constantly dragging me down, and I saw no hope for it to change. It had dominated the space in my mind since childhood. I had no reason to think the problem was ever going to change. But I also felt trapped because I felt there was a tiny lion living inside my heart that wanted to be let loose. I enjoyed my job as a teacher, but I felt like I was just getting comfortable in it. I felt like I was descending as a man.

Near the end of my teaching career, I chaperoned a field trip at a zoo. While there, I came across an enclosure that was about as big as a barn. In the middle of this enclosed area was a tree that spread out and took up much of the space. I couldn't see any creatures, so I read the posted sign. I was surprised to read there was an eagle inside that space. My first thought was, *There is no room for an eagle to spread its wings and fly in this cage.*

In my mind, I spent about two years in conversation with that eagle. As I looked at that eagle, I saw comfort, security, and a good reputation. The eagle is safe. The eagle is fed daily. And every now and then, people stop, look, and are

impressed by the eagle. I felt as though I was living the same life. I was living for security, comfort, and reputation. But there was a question that haunted me: *Hey, Mr. Eagle. What does it feel like to not use your wings?* That is where I was as a man. I had wings, but my life had shrunk around me, and it did not require that I use them.

So, I had a choice. I could keep living for comfort, security, and a good reputation. Or I could let the tiny lion in my heart have his way. I wasn't sure what life would be like outside that cage, but I knew I couldn't stay inside it. After two years of wrestling, I finally left my teaching job.

This exposed me as a man. I no longer had a job that boosted my confidence. I no longer had financial security. I had left my comfort zone. I was living in the wild—and it was wild. It was lonely. It was hard. I was on my own. I knew there was something more in me that wanted to really live. I began the pursuit of these passions, but all along there was a gentle tap on my shoulder I could not escape. Every once in a while, I would sense this nudge. I always felt like I was being reminded of the same thing: *Deal with your weight.* I hated that thought. *I can't do it. Plus, food is really a source of comfort, and life is very uncomfortable right now.* But the tap on my shoulder continued: *Deal with your weight.*

Finally, it happened. I was on a conference call with a group of entrepreneurs. One man spoke up and told his story. He had weighed over three hundred pounds and eventually got down under two hundred pounds. The thought hit me, *I need to talk to that guy.* That day, I reached out to a stranger named Alan Thomas, and we had a conversation. It was one step. And that was the one step I took that brought me out of my bush.

Alan did not talk to me about dieting. He did not talk about an exercise plan. Instead, Alan asked me, "What's holding you back?" This was not the discussion that I had anticipated. This conversation went beneath my problem to my core. I told him what I was really afraid of. I was honest about the real me. The conversation was not about food. It was about me. I was afraid that I was going to die young and that everyone would sit at my funeral and think, *Mark was a good guy. If only he could have stopped eating.* **I was afraid my kids would sit in the front row at my funeral, looking at a man who never showed them what freedom looked like.**

Alan also asked me, "What's it holding you back from?" At that moment, I was not sure what to think of that question. It surprised me. I was not sure what to say. Now I look back and see the magnitude of that question. People who are overweight might think that getting in better shape is the goal. But the story is much bigger than that. Alan opened my mind to the much bigger story. I had looked at my life as if the goal was to gain a smaller body. Alan looked way beyond that and basically asked me what I was made for.

Alan convinced me to get accountability for my journey, so I started a closed group on a social media platform. Every day I posted a picture of my scale. More importantly, I made videos in which I talked to the members of the group about why I weighed what I weighed. **I processed the weight that had accumulated between my ears.** This group gave me an opportunity to continue living outside of the hiding place of that bush.

Your Story

I am overwhelmed with excitement at the thought of you taking this next step. But let me tell you why. I'm excited because *people need you.* You have a gift to offer people. **I am not dreaming of your problem going away. I am dreaming of your purpose being lived out.** I am dreaming of the look in your eyes when you start to live free. The results of freedom come along over the course of time. But I want you to leave the cage you are in. You may have focused on your problem for so long that you are dreaming about that problem being gone. **But what if you started to dream about the difference you can make?**

Fighting for the life I was made for.

#3

*Scan the
QR code
for more*

Here are three thoughts that may be helpful to you right now:

- ***You don't have to believe that your comeback can happen.***
  Sometimes our beliefs are simply feelings we have. Our
  feelings will betray us. They will never be an effective
  driving force to change. The steps we need to take will not
  make sense to our feelings. Do you want feelings, or do you
  want change?

- **You don't have to know how to make it happen.** You will never know how to walk this out before you walk it out. Instinctual logic says, *When I completely understand the ten steps I need to take, I will take the first step.* That sounds useful, and we would all like it if life worked that way. We would all like to come out of hiding with a detailed plan for each step. On top of that, we would like results that are guaranteed. But that is not how life works.

- **You don't have to have the perfect solution.** The perfect solution does not exist. The next diet book proclaims the perfect solution...until you look at the next book after that. We can spend years researching in our prison cell. It seems helpful. But constant research can keep us living in a tiny traffic circle—inside our prison cell. Study does not transform. Action transforms. Do you want information, or do you want transformation?

 ## My Challenge for You

> If there is a story about your life that you are afraid to tell...tell it. That's my challenge for you. Seems simple. Feels awkward. Sounds awful. But consider this: If you are unable to tell this story, it shows how impactful that story is in your life. You might ask, *What's the big deal about telling my story?* The better question is, *If it's not such a big deal, then why am I hiding it?*

Before you tell your story, I want to offer you some wisdom for this step.

- The goal here is to take your problem out of hiding. This is not about studying your problem. Look at this like a weed. Pull it up by its roots and throw it away. Over the course of time, you will have time to process your past, but begin by simply taking it out of hiding.

- I recommend that you do not share your story with a family member. Sometimes people who are close to us are unable to have a balanced perspective concerning our story. You certainly may have someone in your family to whom you can talk about this but be sure to use discretion.

- Talk to someone who seems to be living life free. Sometimes you can perceive that a person is living in a bush. Talking to a person in the bush is talking to someone who has a "bush" mindset. Your experience will be different if you talk with someone who is already free.

CHAPTER 9

What happens When You Come Out of Hiding?

Imagine a little boy who spilled something on the carpet. He knows he was wrong, and he is afraid of the results of his actions. He runs and hides under the bed. He wonders when someone will see his mess. He wonders if they will know he did it. He wonders if he will be found. But there is something he is not realizing. While he is in hiding, his life is on hold. He could be playing. He could go into the backyard to run around, but his life potential is stifled while he lives in hiding.

Messes happen in life. **But the devastation occurs when we allow the mess to steal us away from the pursuit of the life we were made for.** The little boy can learn to face his mess and help clean it up. When we come out of hiding, we get back to living. And dreaming. And playing! We have a life to live and things to do.

My Story

I did not realize what I had become as a man. In the bush, I was compensating as I tried to hide my problem from other people. I did not know how damaging this behavior was. As I maneuvered my life around my problem, I did not realize how impacting it was on others. When people dealt with me, they had to maneuver around the bush I hid behind. Although the bush is invisible to the eye, it can be felt. That is why my relationships became impacted. People didn't realize why things were so awkward with me. And I didn't realize why things were so awkward with other people.

When I came out of the bush, I was surprised at what I could now see about myself. I noticed how judgmental I was about other people. I assumed that everyone who looked at me was judging me by how I looked. Some people probably were because that is what humans tend to do. But I was assuming that everyone was shallow. I was judging people by assuming they were judging me by my appearance.

Maybe the greatest impact of coming out of hiding was that I could see the path of freedom. And I realized I was on it. I saw my life from outside my prison cell. **The path of freedom was joyful and light. I had not lost weight below my shoulders yet, but I had lost the weight that was resting above my shoulders inside my own head. How I saw my problem had created "overweight thinking."**

I started to see the opportunities I had. In hiding, I was only thinking about my problem and making sure nobody else was seeing it. Out of hiding, I started to see my gifts. And I wanted to share my gifts with others. I stopped judging my life by my behavior and what my body looked like. I stopped looking at myself through the lens of my problem. Instead, I saw my life through the lens of the life I was made to live.

Your Story

Maybe you have spent years orienting your life around your pain, your problem, or your past. Isn't it time to orient your life around a different question: What were you made for? In the bush, it appears that the story of our life is the thing that went wrong. But that is not the story of our lives.

In your life, you have faced trouble, just like everyone else. And you will continue to wrestle with weakness, problems, etc. But only one question matters: **Will you be the person you were made to be?** As you are coming out of that bush, I hope you are starting to dream again. I hope your goals are being shaped by who you were made to be.

I hope you followed through on the challenge I gave you in the previous chapter. If you did not, ask yourself why you didn't. Then go back to the end of chapter 8 and look at that challenge again. Your life is worth taking that step. If you did, now think about these questions:

- How do you see your problem now?

- How do you see your past now?

- How do you see yourself now?

- How do you see others now?

 ## My Challenge for You

> Discuss the four questions above with someone else.

CHAPTER 10

Why Is the Journey of Freedom So Messy?

Our desire for life to be neat and problem-free holds us back from living bold and free lives. Human instinct pulls us into the mindset that we must be free of weakness to be able to live free. That sounds right. It sounds like it would be great. We would all love to strut through the door every day, feeling like we are completely prepared for anything that comes at us. We would love to think that nothing about us could possibly be seen in a negative way. We would love to enter every room in our lives with the feeling that we have no flaws.

This thinking undermines our lives. We become people who live to avoid problems instead of being people who look to do good. Because of this thinking, we end up disqualifying ourselves at every turn. Having a problem is not the problem. How we think about our problem is what holds us back. That is why the journey of freedom must be messy. We need the messy journey to mess with our thinking. If our problem was quickly solved, we would still have our wrong ways of thinking.

The messy, imperfect journey is what causes us to uproot our wrong ways of thinking. We may believe the great goal is to live problem-free. That is not the point. The goal is to become a person who uses problems as opportunities. This requires a messy journey. And this makes our problem the greatest opportunity of our life. Without our problem, we simply will not learn this lesson.

My Story

I started to weigh myself every day. I recorded my weight and posted it to a group of about thirty friends on social media. I weighed myself every day because I needed to stop fearing the scale. For years, I had avoided that little square object in my bathroom. Although I had never even stood on it, I was afraid of what it said. I passed by it for most of my life. But it whispered to me every time. The inability to step on that scale shows the lack of freedom I had. So, I started stepping onto that scale every day to prove I was not going to let it determine who I was as a man.

At one point, I looked at the number I had recorded and noticed something interesting. Over the course of about 150 days, I had lost fifty pounds. Many days I gained weight and it appeared I was going in the wrong direction, but over the course of time, I had started crushing it! This is what it looks like in our lives when we face problems. It is a long boxing match. We may lose four rounds in a row, but as long as we keep showing up in the ring, we are going to win.

I needed to fail. Failure was my best teacher. I needed the lessons that occurred through failure. The journey was messy for me. Some days I wondered whether I was changing at all.

On those days, I would go to my closet and pull out an old suit jacket. Just about a year earlier, I could not have buttoned that jacket. But now, I could wrap it around me and almost fit a basketball between my body and the buttoned jacket. That jacket was a reminder to me of my success even when I felt like I was losing.

This messy, imperfect journey was the perfect journey. I needed to change how I thought about myself. I needed to change how I looked at weakness. I needed to change how I thought about others. I needed to change how I thought about God. The journey of losing weight was the greatest education of my life. It still is. I love facing it. It is my greatest gift. **Facing my human weakness is my greatest gift.**

The big problem of my life was not being overweight. The big problem was how I looked at my problem. If I had taken a magic pill and woken up skinny the next day, that would have given me a huge disadvantage. The weight was not the problem. The thinking that I developed because I was overweight was the problem. I will also say that my thinking is what caused me to be overweight to begin with.

Your Story

How do you look at your problem? Do you think you have to fix it before you can live boldly? If you do, you will probably never live boldly. If you need a perfected life to qualify you to pursue your purpose, you will never pursue your purpose. Perfection does not qualify anybody. The desire for perfection will cause us to always feel like we are disqualified.

I believe that honestly facing weakness is what qualifies us to live boldly. As we face weakness, it teaches us. It equips us. We live in a world where people are trying to become impressive in order to make an impact or gain an audience. In reality, we all have an audience. And we can all make an impact. **Facing our weakness with honesty and boldness will equip us for who we were made to be.**

Are you okay if your problem takes a year to overcome? If you are overcoming an addiction, are you okay if you still have a strong desire for whatever it was you were addicted to? If you have had your problem for ten years, you probably need to wrestle with that problem for at least another year. The wrestling with the problem is how you learn the thinking required to live the life you really want to live.

On your journey of freedom, you will fail many times. That does not mean you are still in a prison. This is critical to understand. **In between the prison and the life you are made to live, there will be moments that might feel like prison, or smell like prison.** In these moments, you might think you have not gotten anywhere. For example, if I overate, I would sometimes feel that I was still the same person I had been before. This is an example of how my thinking needed to change. How I eat does not determine my identity. I may overeat, but I am still living free and pursuing my purpose. I don't live in that prison anymore. I may still fail, but I fail while on the path of purpose. My behavior does not determine my identity!

As you embark on your journey of change, imagine how messy it will be. It's okay. Realize you will sometimes lose as much as you win. It's okay. Gauge yourself by the pursuit of your purpose, rather than by whether you are perfect. Every time you fail, realize it is just practice. You are learning how to think differently.

My Challenge for You

Notice the picture. This illustrates what your pathway of freedom will look like. You will be free, but you will also be flawed. Freedom is not about perfection. Remember that your problem did not put you in the prison cell. *The way you thought about your problem* put you in the prison cell. You will have ups and downs on the journey. The key will be what you do in those down moments. With each down moment, you might want to yell at yourself, "Look what I just did! I am still in the bush!" But that is not true. These failures are just messy lessons. They are a necessary part of the journey. These moments give us the opportunity to learn how to see our problem differently.

Here is what I want you to do: Right now, I want you to decide what you are going to do when you hit a down moment. For me, when I felt down, I would go to my closet and get my old suit jacket that used to be too small. Then I would put it on, and it would remind me that I had changed. What will you do when you fail? You might have a friend you can call. You might do something that refreshes you. You might do something to chase your purpose boldly. Think of options right now and record them below.

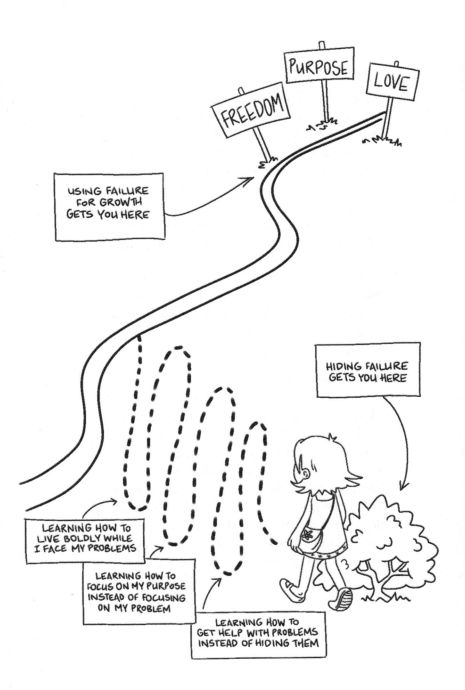

CHAPTER 11

What Is Accountability, and How Does It Help?

Accountability is commonly spoken of as a necessary tool for life change. It is a great tool. But there are many types of accountability that are not helpful. Good accountability requires the right people, the right principles, and the right practices.

The Right People

People who have accomplished what you want to accomplish are the right kind of people. If you want to travel from point A to point F, find someone who has traveled from point A to point F. In my story, Alan Thomas was a guy who at one point had the problem I had. He had overcome being what I was, so it made sense to speak with him. You want to get accountability from people who have traveled the path you need to take.

The Right Principles

There is one principle of accountability that I find is often missed. Normally we see accountability as having people in our lives who help us overcome a problem. Although that seems to be the right goal, there is a more powerful form of accountability. The best form of accountability is having someone who is helping you live out your purpose. This is critical. When a person is pursuing their purpose, they live with a far greater sense of power. Purpose gives us a reason to face our problems. The people who see our purpose, and point us to it, are the best people to hold us accountable. Remember this: Our biggest problem was how we thought about our problem. I love people who help me look at my problem differently. The people in my life who point me to my purpose are the people that I want to talk to about my problem.

The Right Practices

There are many types of help out there for people. Not all of them work. Honestly, the majority of products and services that help people change behaviors and mindsets are designed with good intentions, but many fall short or fail completely. Let's face it, human change is not easy. Hopefully, you are beginning to see and understand that your mindset combined with a process for change is what helps you. If I could summarize it simply, I would say this: Don't fix your problem. Pursue your purpose. Why? Because if you try to "fix yourself," you will multiply your problem and hold your life hostage. As you pursue your purpose, you will gain momentum and power to face your problem. You can live your best bold life while you honestly face your problem.

I would like to tell you a story that demonstrates a practice that helps us to change. It's one of my favorite stories to tell, so I made this video for you.

One thing... one time.

#4

Scan the QR code for more

My Story

I used to think accountability was the weirdest thing. It made no sense to me. I could not understand how another human could help me with my problem. I also had no interest in admitting a personal problem to another person. So, accountability seemed like the perfect way to ruin a friendship. I never tried it.

When I signed up with Alan Thomas to let him help me, he challenged me that I had to find accountability. That was our first argument together. He pushed me on it until I agreed to it. I started a closed group on a social media platform and invited about eight friends to be in the group. I then made a video and told them I was going to tell them two things every day: How much I weighed, and also why I weighed what I weighed.

Every day I unpacked some of my story as I looked into my phone to make that video. I talked about why I was overweight. Every day I was learning something new about myself. I was seeing my problem differently. I was seeing everything differently. I invited more people into the group, and it grew to over seventy people. I now love accountability. I love it because I understand it now. These people in my life were not people who were helping me lose weight. They were cheering me on to fulfill my purpose.

These friends did not call to ask me how much food I was eating. They called to ask me if I was living boldly. I want those calls. I want those people in my life. I want that kind of accountability. When people point me to my purpose, they give me the power to face my problem.

Your Story

I hope you can get excited about having people who become coaches and cheerleaders for your journey. Remember, accountability is not about having people who drill down on your problem and judge you. It is about having people who stand in the corner of your boxing ring and cheer you on.

Someone in your corner needs to have the knowledge for the fight you are in. Many people would like to be cheerleaders for our journey. This is a vital role. But we need to have someone who fills the role of a coach. Allow at least one person to be close enough to smell your breath.

 ## My Challenge for You

There are two things that need to be decided.

1. What is your purpose? It is hard to chase your purpose when you don't know what it is. (I'll talk about this briefly later.) In short, your purpose is not to fix your problem. There must be a stronger reason for change.

2. Who do you want to invite into your journey? Who is the person that has walked your journey ahead of you? It may be a service you pay for. It may be a mentor. It may be a neighbor. Simply look for someone who used to be what you are, but now they have become what you want to become. Reach out to them and ask them to share in your journey. After finding someone to play the role of your coach, you will also invite others to be your cheerleaders. After all, much of accountability is simply having people who cheer you on to keep fighting the fight.

CHAPTER 12

What Is Vulnerability?

Vulnerability is the ability to live boldly in spite of weakness.
This simple thought is life-changing, but it is often misunderstood.
It feels like a test to see if we are willing to do awkward things.
It is far more than that.

Vulnerability is not the ability to embarrass yourself in public.
Vulnerability enables us to offer our best gift in public even
though we are imperfect.

Vulnerability is not the ability to admit your secrets in public.
Vulnerability is the ability to live your life without the constant
effort of hiding your past.

Vulnerability is not the goal of exposing people to our
weaknesses.
Vulnerability is about leading others honestly while we
have weaknesses.

Vulnerability is not about belittling yourself.
Vulnerability is the ability to live your life with the courage to do big things even when you have a mess.

Vulnerability is not about accepting that you are a weak person.
Vulnerability is the ability to live your life in full pursuit of your purpose even though you have weakness.

Vulnerability is not about exposing your problems to people.
Vulnerability is the ability to live your life without living in fear of embarrassment.

Vulnerability is not about being honest with everyone about our problem.
Vulnerability is the ability to live authentically with others.

Vulnerability is not about admitting the problem.
Vulnerability enables us to be able to live boldly instead of living our lives constantly engrossed in our fears, insecurities, problems.

My Story

I was always trying to prove I had no problems. I wanted people to think I had everything together. This sounds prideful. And it is. Living your life to gain the approval or admiration of others is prideful. If I am completely honest, I see many people struggling with this same thing.

I thought the admission of weakness would disqualify me in the eyes of others. That is why I could not admit weakness. I always wanted to belong. I wanted to be an asset to those around me. I wanted my life to make a difference. But I thought these things could not be a reality in my life if I had any weakness. Using a sports metaphor, I thought I would get put on the bench by people. *If people know I have a weakness, they will not see me as someone who can help.* This thinking had me stuck. I could not admit weakness because I felt it would invalidate me. So, all my effort was spent in three different ways. First, hide weakness at all costs. Second, try to prove myself to people by faking it. And third, try to fix my problem. Admittedly, I did not have a lot of time to tackle number three. Numbers one and two consumed my time and gave me no motivation for number three.

This was a frustrating existence. I wasn't able to simply be me. That is probably the core of what freedom is: the ability to boldly be me. No pretending. No walking on eggshells. No longer living like I have to compensate for myself in every conversation. No longer trying to prove something to people.

I learned something interesting. When I became open with people about my weakness, they wanted my help. The old me was always trying to impress people, but I felt like nobody was interested in what I had to say. Now, by being vulnerable, people came close to me. They wanted me. They wanted my gift.

I could not see it then, but I can look back and see it now. My lack of vulnerability had caused me to live behind a wall. People could not get to me. The wall that was hiding my weakness was also preventing people from experiencing *me*. This imaginary wall was blocking my relationship with others.

When I stopped hiding my one big problem, I gained the ability to stop fearing all of my problems. That is why vulnerability matters. It's not because of that one hidden problem. It is because the bigger problem is the fear of problems. Fear of what people think. Fear of messing up. Fear of something going wrong.

Your Story

If you are like me, the thought of vulnerability does not sound appealing. It sounds awkward and weak. It sounds like you have become a person who walks around timidly. No. No. And no! Vulnerability does not put you on the sidelines to live a passive existence. Vulnerability gives you the ability to live your best life even while you have weakness. Vulnerability is how Clark Kent puts the cape around his neck. Without vulnerability, the super-hero waits until he has no kryptonite before he rescues anyone.

Vulnerability is a preacher speaking in front of an audience. He is proclaiming big truths even while he struggles with his own weakness. Vulnerability enables a boxer to go into a ring and fight. He could get knocked out. He cannot guarantee his safety. Vulnerability enables two young people to stand at an altar and pledge their love to each other. They do not know what the road will look like, but they want to take this journey together into the unknown.

Vulnerability is the ability that allows someone to start a business. There are no guarantees of success, and failure is certainly an option, but some things are simply worth attempting. Vulnerability is found in a woman who decides to have a baby. She does not know what the process will be like inside of her. She cannot control what's happening in her body, but it gives her such a beautiful gift in the end.

Do you know what it's like to live *without* vulnerability? Instead of having the guts to pursue a dream, we live to avoid nightmares. Without vulnerability, the goal is to not mess up. We become a constant judge of ourselves. The fears of life multiply as we live to avoid them.

This lack of vulnerability hinders those around us. Those closest to us are forced to live inside of our fears. Because we are afraid of messing up, we also become afraid of them messing up. In our attempt to protect their life, we block their life. We think we are keeping them safe, but we end up keeping them from living. We train our kids to fear. We need them to live a life that makes us feel secure. **Living in the shadow of our insecurities, they learn to fear failure.**

Great love—*real* love—requires vulnerability. Without vulnerability, I lose my capacity to be a great lover to my own spouse. I judge their behavior instead of empowering their life. Without vulnerability, I hide weakness from my spouse. As I hide my weakness from them, I also hide my gift from them. As I hide weakness from others, I cannot see the imaginary wall that forms between me and those I want to love. They want to love me, but they are too afraid of messing up with me.

Human weakness will always be a part of our lives. Every part of our life contains weakness. **Vulnerability allows these areas of weakness to be useful in our life instead of seeing areas of weakness as a threat to our life.** Vulnerability unlocks the power of your weakness. Weakness will either define you and hold you back, or it can be a tool to refine you and move you forward.

 ## My Challenge for You

This life of powerful vulnerability cannot happen without relationships with others. We need to have people in our life who fully know us, yet fully believe in us. We need to be around people who know our weaknesses, but they see our gifts as being far greater. We can tell them our problems, but they just keep pointing us toward our purpose. My challenge for you is to find your people. They are out there. They want the gift of you. And you need the gift of them.

Here is another challenge. Human instinct causes us to try to do impressive things to move forward in life. Instead, look for *vulnerable* things to do. Here are some examples: admit your weakness to someone, weigh yourself, go to the doctor for a physical, ask someone out on a date, invite friends over to your house even though it's messy, ask for help with a project that is hard for you, join a workout class at the gym, sign up for a church group, ask someone for advice, forgive someone who hurt you, etc.

Allow me for just a second to put my hand on your shoulder and tell you how important it is to take these vulnerable steps. They are awkward. They take us out of our comfort zone. **These vulnerable steps do not seem powerful, but they change our thinking.** It is outside of our comfort zone that we experience the things we really want in life.

CHAPTER 13

Why Does Purpose Matter?

We were not born to be problem-free. You were born to boldly live out a purpose in this world. Purpose is a powerful motivator. Purpose gives us a reason to live. Purpose enables us to see our problems in the correct light. In terms of our purpose, there are two foundational ways of looking at the relationship between our problems and our purpose.

The most **common mindset** is that *I can't have a powerful purpose until I get rid of this awful problem.* That is the default mindset for most of us. But there is a different mindset that we can have. I call it a **redemptive mindset**. This mindset enables us to think, *I have a powerful purpose, and facing my problem becomes a sharpening stone for the sword of my purpose.*

The common mindset is a full-time trail of frustration: *As soon as my problem is fixed, I will have a purpose!* This sounds moral, but it gives us no power. The redemptive mindset allows us to have the boldness to race after our purpose even while we have a problem in our life.

COMMON MINDSET

REDEMPTIVE MINDSET

The common mindset causes us to wake up every day to avoid something, while the redemptive mindset enables us to wake up every day and pursue something. This is why knowing our purpose is so important. If I do not know my purpose, I will default to the common mindset of focusing on my problem.

My Story

I was not born to be skinny. I was born to be free. I was born to love people. I was born for a purpose. I was born to do something with my life, not just wear a particular size of clothes. As I focused on my problem, I was holding my purpose hostage.

When I brought my problem out of hiding, it brought my purpose out of hiding as well. When I came out of hiding, it allowed me to have a different perspective on my life. I saw that

I didn't have to spend my days hating and hiding my problem. Instead, I could pursue my purpose with boldness every day. I don't have to wait. **I don't have to fix myself first. I can live out my purpose right now.**

Purpose gave me power. I realized that pursuing my purpose was how I could win at life. When I tried to fix my problem, I was focusing on how I was losing at life. But the only way to change the scoreboard was to chase my purpose. This was a completely different way of looking at life. It was liberating. I stopped tracking how I was failing, and I started tracking my purpose! **I did not need my body to become smaller before I lived a life that was bigger.**

I was only thinking about the problem in me instead of my purpose for others. I was trying to drive my life with the fuel of overcoming my problem. That fuel does not last. Instead, I saw how I had something to offer to others. And I started offering it. Pursuing my purpose gave me the fuel I needed.

A number of things began to happen:

1. My relationship with my wife became better than ever. I became a different person for her. She loved this new version of me. I used to always hide my weakness, and live in shame. But when I admitted weakness, I took the bag off my head. Numerous times she told me, "Thank you for giving me all of you." She loved watching me pursue my purpose, and she was attracted to my vulnerability.

2. My relationships with others changed. I used to wonder what people thought about my problem. Now I think about how I can help them. I was able to share openly about who I was because I wasn't hiding anymore. And a crazy thing happened. As I shared my weakness, they saw my gift. I had spent a lifetime thinking that if I was honest about my

weakness, people would disqualify me. I thought if people really knew me, they would reject me. The truth is, as I was honest and open about my weakness, it enabled people to know me fully. And love me fully. And I found that people loved me. And they wanted me. **It doesn't make sense, but as I showed my weakness, they saw my gift.**

3. I was able to help people. I look back at my life and think about how I have always wanted to help people. But I never let people help me. As I was honest about my weakness and allowed people to help me, I gained wisdom for how to help other people. I never thought I would be able to help people with addiction, depression, anxiety, and marriage problems. But that is happening now.

4. A business was created. I was never a person who thought about starting a business. There were a couple of reasons for this. First, I just didn't think that way. I was never a person who had an entrepreneurial mindset. Second, I was too busy thinking about my problems. I did not have the ability to dream about what I could do. Long story short, we started a business. My wife and I now do this full-time together. This was never the goal or the plan, but I look back and see this simple equation for life. Know your purpose + honestly face your weakness + do it all with others.

Your Story

My friend, I wish we were face-to-face for the words that I want to say to you right now. *You have a purpose. People need you.* This book is not about you making your problem smaller. It's about you living a bigger life. And you can live out that life now.

Although we have not met yet, can I be very bold with you? I know what's wrong with you. Can I tell you? *Nothing!* Nothing is wrong with you. You may have a mess, but you are not a mess. You may have multiple messes, but you are not a mess.

You can stop trying to fix yourself. Go and be yourself. Pursue your purpose. The pursuit of your purpose will give you fuel for your entire life. Face your weakness. But chase your purpose. Go to counseling if you want. Sign up for the gym if you want. Hire a coach. Get practical help with your weakness—but chase your purpose.

As you read this, you might be like I used to be. The topic of purpose may seem like it is for other people. You might feel like you are not worthy of purpose. This is not the truth. Your problems have been standing in front of you and lying to you. They have spoken to you for long enough. Although your problems have had a real impact in your real life, you can leave behind the lies that your problems told you.

- You have a purpose.

- You can know your purpose.

- It's not too late for you.

- You have not messed up too much.

I met with a man a few months ago who was drinking heavily. He initially admitted his drinking issue, but that was the last we spoke of it. We had four meetings. I sent him a text message after several months to see how he was doing. I asked him, "If a friend told you they were struggling with alcohol, what would you tell them?" Here was his response:

Man, I have so many answers for that one. I think first I'd say you've been tricked, I believe tricked by the devil himself, into believing that with a little numbing, you can be okay with not being all you could be. With just settling in and making no impact and not living life as you were created to live it. I think when you know why God created you, the devil doesn't like that. If he can convince you that it's easier to just be okay with being mediocre, and numb to who it hurts or affects, then you can't pursue your God-given purpose. I think that numbness convinces you you're not really anything special, you don't have a cool purpose like others do, and it's a lot easier to just accept that than get off your butt and attack life ferociously. But it doesn't take long after lifting that fog and numbness before you realize that pursuing what you were made for is why we exist. Purpose is a beautiful word. I'd rather attack a purpose with everything I have than just exist. We live in a world of blurred lines, where people kind of just want to float along until their time is up. But I don't think we were designed that way. At least I wasn't. I can't wake up and just wonder what I should do today. I want to wake up with goals. Using the metaphors we've talked about before, I want to wake up like a lion, but not like a lion on a substance that numbs reality like a lion at the zoo. I want to wake up like a lion that is ready to hunt! Not pace around being okay with being caged up.

My friend, your problem might be really bothering you. Maybe it has been messing with you for many years. But hear me out on this. I am imagining myself sitting across from you right now, and here is what I am going to say to you: "What are you made for? It doesn't matter where you have been, or what you have done. It does not matter what your habits are. *What are you made for?"*

The greatest result of your life will not be fixing your problem. The greatest result will be your purpose pursued. Facing your problem will help you pursue that purpose more boldly.

 # My Challenge for You

The human heart is not most devastated by the presence of a problem. The human heart is more devastated by the absence of purpose. If you have read this chapter and think, *I don't know my purpose, you may want to reach out to us.* We take people through an experience called "The Purpose Mastermind." This is a journey that enables people to clarify their purpose once and for all. If you want to take the step to clarify your purpose, and you want our help, please reach out.

Here are the ways that you can reach us.

To work with Mark personally:
mark@markdelaney.me

To work with Adena personally:
adena@markdelaney.me

To work with one of the other purpose mastermind facilitators:
visit www.purposemastermind.com.

A Note from the Author

I am not able to complete this work without including the following thoughts. In this book, my goal has been to articulate a pathway to freedom. I have attempted to describe what it looks like in our real lives. But I must tell you where this understanding of freedom comes from. This freedom that I have described comes from the pages of Scripture.

For many people, the Bible is very confusing. Ultimately, the story of the Scriptures lays out a pathway that enables a person to understand how to make sense of their life in a complex world.

The Bible contains the story of how we become lost in the journey of life. But it also shows the pathway to full redemption. One of the first stories we read is about Adam and Eve. They were described as "naked and unashamed." Now, that is freedom! Imagine being so caught up in your life that you don't even notice your nakedness?

Adam and Eve were living a bold life. They were bold and free in their relationship with God and with each other. But then something went wrong, and their perspective completely changed. In a moment, they went into the bushes to hide. They hid from God and covered themselves in shame from each other. Consider the difference in how they lived their life. They went from being bold and free to being ashamed and trapped in their own existence.

They had lost the life they were made to live. They had lost the ability to be who they were made to be. This is the story of all our lives. But the story does not have to end this way for you and me. In the pages of Scripture, we find this pathway to freedom.

Jesus tells a parable about a prodigal son. This son had decided that he wanted to live life his way. He ventured out from his father's life, but he quickly ruined himself. He found himself living in a pigpen. This pigpen was his bush. He had to take a very vulnerable step to gain freedom. He had to go home and stand before his family in nothing but the filth and disgrace of what his life had become.

Then the prodigal son took the one step to freedom. He did not fix himself. He did not atone for what he had done. He did not earn his way back home. He simply crawled. He came home with nothing but the honesty of who he really was.

In this parable, we see the beautiful response of his father. His father ran to him and put a robe around his neck. (I like to think of it as a cape!) He put a ring on his finger. In his father's response, you get a glimpse as to how he saw his son. He did not ask his son, "Why did you do those things?" Instead, he quickly reminded his son of what he was made for. He pointed him toward his purpose. The father was unfazed at how his son had messed up. He saw what his son was made for. In his son's most vulnerable moment before the world, the father proclaimed a bold message to him. He demonstrated to his son that it does not matter where you have been, or what you have done. When he ran to his son and put the robe around his neck, he was declaring, "You are my son. I love you, and I'm going to remind you of who you were made to be."

This simple, yet powerful story shows us the story of our own lives. We are all the prodigal at some point. We are lost and broken. When things break down, we quickly lose sight of three things:

1. We lose sight of how we got to this point.

2. We lose sight of how to get out of this broken place.

3. We lose sight of who we were made to be to begin with.

My friend, the Gospel of Jesus Christ offers the ultimate freedom pathway for all mankind. Jesus came to set us free from the need to save ourselves. We can humbly come out of the bushes of a fake life. We can replace compensating and hiding with freedom and purpose. **We can't fix the wreckage, but we can walk away from it.**

At the end of Jesus' teaching, we find an interesting twist. Jesus told this parable, but He did not end after the dramatic scene with the son coming home. Instead, Jesus used the whole parable to teach something profound to the people who were listening. He pointed everyone to a third person in the parable. The prodigal son's older brother had a far different perspective on the prodigal son. He was not pleased at the return of his brother. He was bitter, jealous, and judgmental. Jesus was making a bold point to those He taught that day. He was warning them to not be like the older brother.

Why did this matter so much? Put yourself in the place of the prodigal son as he made the journey home. What would have happened if the prodigal son had come home and spoken to his older brother first? The conversation would have been very different. The older brother might have said things like this:

- "How could you do what you did?"

- "How could you just show up around here again?"

- "How did you waste all the money?"

- "You know that nobody wants to see you!"

- "You need to go earn back the money first!"

- "It's going to take a long time for you to earn back our trust!"

The prodigal would have turned around and walked right back to the pigpen he'd been in. Consider this: On the long journey from the pigpen to your people, it's natural to fear how people will respond. You don't feel worthy. You feel undeserving of grace. If I was the prodigal, and I had met my brother for that kind of conversation, I would just turn around and walk back to where I came from.

Human instinct is to think like the prodigal's older brother. We seem to think that if we are hard enough on people, they will change. If I threaten them enough. If I warn them enough. If I yell loud enough. If I judge them enough, they will change. If I show them how disgusted I am at their problem, they will change.

The father in this parable represents the love of God for humanity. Through the sacrifice of Jesus on the cross, there is a pathway to freedom. This freedom does not come through human effort. Just like in this story, the prodigal simply had to humble himself to receive this redemption.

This redemption brings the power to change. This redemption comes with complete forgiveness from our past and a powerful purpose for our future. Redemption means *I am completely free and able to pursue my purpose.* Without redemption, we think we have to earn the right to be forgiven and earn the right to have a purpose.

The prodigal son is now fully accepted. But you may wonder, *What about the mess he created?* Redemption means *I'm forgiven.* It means *I am restored to full membership in the family.* It means *I can pursue my best, bold life.* This means the prodigal son can wear his robe proudly, live his purpose boldly—**and honestly face the mess he caused.** Facing the mess he created will sharpen the sword of his purpose.

The prodigal can have an honest conversation with his family about what he has done. Because he is a brother and a son, he will apologize. He will work to restore the financial loss that hindered the family. **But he does this because he has been restored. He does not do this *in order to be* restored.**

I would like to finish with one more story from the pages of Scripture. But I would like to say this to you face-to-face. Check out the QR code for this story.

Do you love me...feed my sheep
#5

Scan the QR code for more